Heartwarming Thoughts for Moms

BARBOUR
PUBLISHING

The Simple Things in Life

When we take time to notice the simple things in life, we never lack for encouragement. We discover we are surrounded by limitless hope that's just wearing everyday clothes.

— ANONYMOUS

Trust Him

God tells us in His Word that worry is a profitless activity. Worrying about our children may feel like a natural thing to do, but in reality it's sin. If we are constantly worrying about our kids, it's like saying to God, "I know that You created the universe, but I'm not sure You know what's best for my children. So, I'll handle them, God."

— MICHELLE MEDLOCK ADAMS

Hold Us Close

God of the years that lie behind us, Lord of the
years that stretch before, Weaver of all the ties
that bind us, Keeper and King of the open door:
through all seasons—planting and reaping,
all through the harvest of song and tears,
hold us close in Your tender keeping,
O Maker of all New Years!

—ANONYMOUS

One Life

We have just one life, and our Savior died and rose again so that it could be an abundant life. When Jesus said in John 10:10 (NIV), "I have come that they may have life, and have it to the full," He wasn't talking about a day planner jam-packed with activities or a schedule crammed with "to-do's." Christ was speaking about a life of purpose, contentment, and peace.

—DENA DYER

When God Thought of Mother

When God thought of mother, he must have laughed with satisfaction, and framed it quickly—so rich, so deep, so divine, so full of soul, power, and beauty was the conception!

—HENRY WARD BEECHER

What Is a Home?

What is home? A roof to keep out the rain?
Four walls to keep out the wind? Floors to keep out
the cold? Yes, but home is more than that. It is the
laugh of a baby, the song of a mother. . .warmth
of loving hearts, lights from happy eyes, kindness,
loyalty, comradeship. Home is first school and first
church for young ones, where they learn what is
right, what is good, and what is kind.

— ANONYMOUS

To Manage Children

In order to manage children well, we must borrow
their eyes and their hearts, see and feel as they do,
and judge them from their own point of view.

—Eugenie de Guerin

God Gave Us Mothers

God gave us Mothers because He knew
There are some things only Mothers can do.
Stories just she knows that need to be told;
Hugs that get born in a heart made of gold.
God sends us so many things from above,
Delivered by Mothers wrapped up in love.

— ANONYMOUS

Take Time for Make-Believe

Take time for make-believe. Abandon yourself in play. I think God gives us an imagination for a reason. Christ knows the pressures we endure. Perhaps this is one reason He encourages us to "become as little children."

— JEAN LUSH WITH PAM VREDEVELT

The Eyes of a Mother

When you looked into my mother's eyes you knew, as if He had told you, why God had sent her into the world. . .it was to open the minds of all who looked to beautiful things.

— JAMES M. BARRIE

Virtues

Pride is one of the seven deadly sins; but it cannot be the pride of a mother in her children, for that is a compound of two cardinal virtues—faith and hope.

— CHARLES DICKENS

An Angel on Earth

My mother was an angel on earth. She was a
minister of blessings to all human beings within her
sphere of action. Her heart was the abode
of heavenly purity.

— JOHN QUINCY ADAMS

In God's Eyes

What seem our worst prayers may really be,
in God's eyes, our best. Those, I mean, which are
least supported by devotional feeling. For these
may come from a deeper level than feeling.
God sometimes seems to speak to us most intimately
when He catches us, as it were, off our guard.

— C. S. LEWIS

Day 14

Love Never Fails

Love never fails. But where there is talking back, it will—eventually—cease. (Please, Lord?) Where there is a teenager who thinks she knows everything, there will come an adult who knows you did your best. For we know we fail our children, and we pray that they don't end up in therapy. But when we get to heaven, our imperfect parenting will disappear. (Thank God!) And now these three remain: faith, hope, and love. But the greatest of these is. . .a mother's love.

— DENA DYER

Motherhood

Motherhood:
All love begins and ends there—
roams enough,
But, having run the circle, rests at home.

— ROBERT BROWNING

Mothers Help

A little boy's mother once told him that it is God who makes people good. He looked up and replied, "Yes, I know it is God; but mothers help a lot."

— UNKNOWN

A Precious Gift

An inexhaustible good nature is one of the most precious gifts of heaven, spreading itself like oil over the troubled sea of thought, and keeping the mind smooth and equable in the roughest weather.

— WASHINGTON IRVING

His Goodness

God has given you your child, that the sight of
him, from time to time, might remind you of
His goodness, and induce you to praise Him
with filial reverence.

— CHRISTIAN SCRIVER

Mother

"M" is for the million things she gave me,
"O" means only that she's growing old,
"T" is for the tears were shed to save me,
"H" is for her heart of purest gold;
"E" is for her eyes, with love-light shining,
"R" means right, and right she'll always be,
Put them all together, they spell MOTHER,
A word that means the world to me.

— HOWARD JOHNSON

Living Water

But whosoever drinketh of the water that I shall give him
shall never thirst; but the water that I shall give him shall
be in him a well of water springing up into everlasting life.

—JOHN 4:14 KJV

First Stories

Stories first heard at a mother's knee are never wholly forgotten—a little spring that never quite dries up in our journey through scorching years.

— GIOVANNI RUFFINI

Be Silent

How can you expect God to speak in that gentle and inward voice which melts the soul, when you are making so much noise. . . ? Be silent and God will speak again.

— FRANÇOIS FÉNELON

No Stronger Bond

There is no love, like a mother's love,
no stronger bond on earth. . .
like the precious bond that comes from God,
to a mother, when she gives birth.

——JILL LEMMING

The Power of Inspiration

My mother. . .taught me about the power of inspiration and courage, and she did it with a strength and a passion that I wish could be bottled.

—— CARLY FIORINA

The Profession of Motherhood

Though motherhood is the most important of all the professions—requiring more knowledge than any other department in human affairs—there was no attention given to preparation for this office.

— ELIZABETH CADY STANTON

Your Strength Shall Be Supplied

The same God who guides the stars in their courses, who directs the earth in its orbit, who feeds the burning furnace of the sun and keeps the stars perpetually burning with their fires— the same God has promised to supply thy strength.

— CHARLES SPURGEON

While We're Not Looking. . .

I hope my children look back on today,
And see a mom who had time to play.
There will be years for cleaning and cooking,
For children grow up while we're not looking.

— ANONYMOUS

Everything for God

What a relief to simply let go of my need to do everything perfectly—and instead just do everything for You, [God]! You know I'll always make mistakes; You know that sometimes my best efforts will look like failures to everybody else. Thank You that I can simply relax and trust You to work everything out according to Your plan.

— DARLENE SALA

The Best You Can Be

My mom taught me to be the best person you can be. Strive to live your life to the fullest and don't let one day go by without trying to live it the best way you can.

— UNKNOWN

Tender Words

When you lead your sons and daughters in the good way, let your words be tender and caressing, in terms of discipline that wins the heart's assent.

— ELIJAH BEN SOLOMON ZALMAN

Only One Mother

Most of all the other beautiful things in life come
by twos and threes, by dozens and hundreds.
Plenty of roses, stars, sunsets, rainbows,
brothers and sisters, aunts and cousins,
but only one mother in the whole world.

— KATE DOUGLAS WIGGIN

Precious Souls

I'll show my children right from wrong, encourage dreams
and hope; explain respect for others, while teaching them
to cope with outside pressures, inside fears, a world that's
less than whole; and through it all I'll nurture my children's
most precious souls!

— ANONYMOUS

Strong and Unyielding

A mother's love is so strong and unyielding
that it usually endures all circumstances——
good fortune and misfortune, prosperity and
privation, honor and disgrace.

—— UNKNOWN

The Shepherd Guides Us

Left to our own agendas, we either run at breakneck speeds right past the pasture. . .or sit in the parched desert. The Shepherd. . .intervenes on our behalf to guide us. . .onto a quiet path and into a calmer faith.

— Patsy Clairmont

Day 35

Rest, Don't Quit

When things go wrong, as they sometimes will,
When the road you're trudging seems all uphill,
When the funds are low and the debts are high,
And you want to smile, but you have to sigh,
When care is pressing you down a bit,
Rest, if you must—but don't you quit!

— ANONYMOUS

Women's Eyes

From women's eyes this doctrine I derive:
They sparkle still the right Promethean fire;
They are the books, the arts, the academes,
That show, contain, and nourish all the world.

— WILLIAM SHAKESPEARE

Home Is the Happiest Place

It ought to enter into the domestic policy of every mother to make her children feel that home is the happiest place in the world. This delicious home-feeling is one of the choicest gifts a parent can bestow.

— Anonymous

God's Greatest Creation

I affirm my profound belief that God's greatest creation is womanhood. I also believe that there is no greater good in all the world than motherhood. The influence of a mother in the lives of her children is beyond calculation.

— JAMES E. FAUST

The Happiest Heart

The happiest heart that ever beat
Was in some quiet breast
That found the common daylight sweet
And left to Heaven the rest.

—JOHN V. CHENEY

God's Love

As high as heaven is over the earth, so strong is his love to those who fear him. And as far as sunrise is from sunset, he has separated us from our sins. As parents feel for their children, God feels for those who fear him.

— Psalm 103:11–13 msg

Wholly Devoted

My mother, whose disposition was always
bright and optimistic, was active,
energetic and wholly devoted to her large family.
No sacrifice was too great, no task too hard,
for her willing heart and hands.

— OSWALD J. SMITH

Unselfish Love

You may have others who will be more
demonstrative but never who will love you more
unselfishly than your mother or who will be
willing to do or bear more for your good.

— CATHERINE BRAMWELL BOOTH

Interruptions Are Opportunities

It may be one more request than we think we can fulfill, one more responsibility than we think we can manage. . . . Interruptions never distracted Jesus. He accepted them as opportunities of a richer service.

— RUTH BELL GRAHAM

A Mother. . .

A mother has the special gift of always speaking true.
A mother gets the praise or blame if skies be dark or blue.
A mother is a doctor, a joiner, or a vet,
The jobs a mother cannot do have not been heard of yet.
Whatever else she may be, a mother knows full well,
A house could never be a home without her magic spell.

— UNKNOWN

The Greatest Virtues

There is no doubt that it is around the family and the home that all the greatest virtues, the most dominating virtues of human society, are created, strengthened, and maintained.

— WINSTON CHURCHILL

A Day of Love

"I love you more than a million red M&Ms."
That's one of our favorite lines from the movie
What a Girl Wants. My daughters and I have
come up with a few of our own "Love you
more thans…" Make today a day of love.
Find new ways to say you love your children.
Then, have each child come up with a new
way to express love to our heavenly Father.

— MICHELLE MEDLOCK ADAMS

Children Are What Matter

One day, when your children are grown and gone,
you'll have time for a perfect house. What matters
now is not the house, but the home; and not the
children's duties, but the children.

— LINDA DAVIS ZUMBEHL

The Last Glimpse

They always looked back before turning the corner, for their mother was always at the window to nod and smile, and wave her hand at them. Somehow it seemed as if they couldn't have got through the day without that, for whatever their mood might be, the last glimpse of that motherly face was sure to affect them like sunshine.

— LOUISA MAY ALCOTT

The Hearth of Home

The house is old, the trees are bare,
Moonless above bends twilight's dome;
But what on earth is half so dear,
So longed for, as the hearth of home?

— EMILY BRONTË

A Mother's Love Is Endless

A mother's love is like a circle. It has no beginning and no ending. It keeps going around and around, ever expanding, touching everyone who comes in contact with it.

— UNKNOWN

A Mother Dreams Our Dreams

A mother laughs our laughs, sheds our tears,
returns our love, fears our fears. She lives our joys,
cares our cares, and all our hopes
and dreams she shares.

— UNKNOWN

A Beautiful Life

How can you live sweetly amid the vexatious things,
the irritating things, the multitude of little worries and
frets, which lie all along your way, and which you cannot
evade? . . . You can live a beautiful life in the midst of
your present circumstances.

—J. R. Miller

One of God's Richest Blessings

One of God's richest blessings, and one of my favorite ironies, is that our children come into the world as people we're supposed to guide and direct, and then God uses them to form us—if we will only listen.

— DENA DYER

One Lamp

One lamp—thy mother's love—amid the stars
Shall lift its pure flame changeless, and before
The throne of God, burn through eternity—
Holy—as it was lit and lent thee here.

— NATHANIEL PARKER WILLIS

The Look of Love

Mother
In her eyes the look of loving,
In her smile the warmth of caring.
In her hands the touch of comfort,
In her heart the gift of sharing.

— UNKNOWN

The Force of Love

There is nothing so strong as the force of love;
there is no love so forcible as the love of an
affectionate mother to her child.

— ELIZABETH GRYMESTON

Only a Mother's Faith

There are times when only a Mother's faith
Can help us on life's way
And inspire in us the confidence
We need from day to day.

— UNKNOWN

Success

To laugh often and much;
To win the respect of intelligent people and the
affection of children;
To appreciate beauty, to find the best in others;
To know even one life has breathed easier
because you have lived.
This is to have succeeded.

— RALPH WALDO EMERSON

An Instrument of Peace

Lord, make me an instrument of Thy peace;
where there is hatred, let me sow love; where there
is injury, pardon; where there is doubt, faith; where
there is despair, hope; where there is darkness, light;
and where there is sadness; joy.

— ST. FRANCIS OF ASSISI

Steep Yourself

Steep yourself in God-reality, God-initiative,
God-provisions. You'll find all your everyday human
concerns will be met. Don't be afraid of missing out.
You're my dearest friends! The Father wants to give you
the very kingdom itself.

— LUKE 12:31–32 MSG

Tomorrow Is a New Day

Finish each day and be done with it. You have done what you could. Some blunders and absurdities no doubt crept in; forget them as soon as you can. Tomorrow is a new day; begin it well and serenely and with too high a spirit to be encumbered with your old nonsense.

— RALPH WALDO EMERSON

"This Is Me"

Each time you pick a daffodil
Or gather violets on some hill
Or touch a leaf or see a tree,
It's all God whispering, "This is Me."

— HELEN STEINER RICE

Day 63

What You Sow

A mother has, perhaps, the hardest earthly lot;
and yet no mother worthy of the name ever gave
herself thoroughly for her child who did not feel that,
after all, she reaped what she had sown.

— HENRY WARD BEECHER

Nothing Can Compare

A mother's love for her child is like nothing else in the world. It knows no law, no pity, it dares all things and crushes down remorselessly all that stands in its path.

— AGATHA CHRISTIE

Just in Sight

They might not need me;
but they might.
I'll let my head be just in sight;
A smile as small as mine might be
Precisely their necessity.

— EMILY DICKINSON

Christ Dwells in Me

I know Christ dwells within me all the time,
guiding me and inspiring me whenever I do
or say anything—a light of which I caught
no glimmer before it comes to me at the very
moment when it is needed.

— St. Therese of Lisieux

Planting Seeds

Upon the mother devolves the duty of planting in the hearts of her children those seeds of love and virtue which shall develop useful and happy lives. There are no words to express the relation of mother to her children.

— A. E. Davis

Who Will Love You Forever?

Who is it that loves me and will love me forever with an affection which no change, no misery, no crime of mine can do away?—It is you, my mother.

— THOMAS CARLYLE

Like the Forest

A mother is a font and spring of life,
A mother is a forest in whose heart
Lies hid a secret ancient as the hills,
For men to claim and take its wealth away;
And like the forest shall her wealth renew
And give, and give again, that men may live.

— FRANCIS CARDINAL SPELLMAN

What Makes a Home?

The Bible does not say very much about homes; it says a great deal about the things that make them. It speaks about life and love and joy and peace and rest. If we get a house and put these into it, we shall have secured a home.

— JOHN HENRY JOWETT

My Wonderful Mother

You are a wonderful mother,
dear old Mother of mine.
You'll hold a spot down deep in my heart,
Till the stars no longer shine.
For there'll never be another to me,
Like that wonderful Mother of mine.

— CLYDE HAGER

Someone to Live For

My mother was the making of me. She was so true and so sure of me, I felt that I had someone to live for—someone I must not disappoint. The memory of my mother will always be a blessing to me.

— THOMAS A. EDISON

A Mother's Role

There is no more influential or powerful role on earth than a mother's. Their words are never fully forgotten, their touch leaves an indelible impression, and the memory of their presence lasts a lifetime.

— CHARLES SWINDOLL

A Living Expression

Let no one ever come to you without leaving
better and happier. Be the living expression of
God's kindness: kindness in your face,
kindness in your eyes, kindness in your smile.

— MOTHER TERESA

I Can Share

There isn't much that I can do,
but I can share my love with you,
and I can share my life with you,
and oftentimes share a prayer with you,
as on our way we go.

— ANONYMOUS

A Precious Gift

There have been many days when God has brought me peace with little, but important, treasures in the midst of a dark mood. But I've found that it's up to me to recognize them and to not let them float away before whispering, "Thanks." Otherwise, I'll have turned away a precious gift.

— DENA DYER

Led by God

I seem to have been led, little by little, toward my work; and I believe that the same fact will appear in the life of anyone who will cultivate such powers as God has given him, and then go on, bravely, quietly, but persistently, doing such work as comes to his hands.

— FANNY CROSBY

Unspeakable Love

There is a sacredness in tears. They are not
the mark of weakness, but of power.
They speak more eloquently than ten
thousand tongues. They are the messengers of
overwhelming grief, of deep contrition,
and of unspeakable love.

— WASHINGTON IRVING

Day 79

Take Time

Take time in your day to be inspired by something
small—the scent of a flower from your garden,
a hug from a child, an "I love you" from your
spouse. . . . Then thank God for the
little things in life.

— FROM *IN THE KITCHEN WITH
MARY AND MARTHA: ONE-DISH WONDERS*

Think on These Things

Finally, beloved, whatever is true, whatever is honorable,
whatever is just, whatever is pure, whatever is pleasing,
whatever is commendable, if there is any excellence and if
there is anything worthy of praise, think about these things.

— PHILIPPIANS 4:8 NRSV

The Spirit of Love

You will find, as you look back upon your life,
that the moments when you have really lived are
the moments when you have done things in the
spirit of love.

— HENRY DRUMMOND

Most Precious Ornament

Mother—in this consists the glory and the most precious ornament of woman.

— Martin Luther

The Love of a Family

Through the eyes of our family, we learn to see ourselves. . .through the love of our family, we learn to love ourselves. . .through the caring of our family, we learn what it means to be ourselves completely.

— ANONYMOUS

My Greatest Wealth

My greatest wealth is the deep stillness in which I strive
and grow and win what the world cannot take from me
with fire and sword.

— JOHANN WOLFGANG VON GOETHE

The Unknown Step

When you come to the edge of all the light you have and you must take a step into that darkness of the unknown, believe that one of two things will happen. Either there will be something for you to stand on or you will be taught how to fly.

— PATRICK OVERTON

An Instant of Pure Love

An instant of pure love is more precious to God. . .
than all other good works together,
even though it may seem as if nothing were done.

— St. John of the Cross

How God Loves Us!

Blue skies with white clouds on summer days.
A myriad of stars on clear moonlit nights.
Tulips and roses and violets and dandelions and
daisies. Bluebirds and laughter and sunshine and
Easter. See how [God] loves us!

— ALICE CHAPIN

Perfect Security

When prayer is at its highest we wait in silence for God's voice
to us; we linger in His presence for His peace and His power
to flow over us and around us; we lean back in His everlasting
arms and feel the serenity of perfect security in Him.

— WILLIAM BARCLAY

Solitude

Solitude replenishes and refreshes us.
It's a necessary and often overlooked facet of a
grace-full life. . . . Pearl S. Buck once said:
"I love people. I love my family, my children. . .
but inside myself is a place where I live all
alone and that's where you renew your springs
that never dry up."

— DENA DYER

In His Hand

Hidden in the hollow of His blessed hand,
Never foe can follow, never traitor stand;
Not a surge of worry, not a shade of care,
Not a blast of hurry, touch the spirit there.

— FRANCES RIDLEY HAVERGAL

Worthwhile

Instead of focusing on the yucky part of cleanup,
remember that the dirty pots and pans, the sticky
table, the crumbs on the floor. . .all mean that you
have a family who needs your love and care.
Now doesn't that just make it all worthwhile?

— FROM *IN THE KITCHEN WITH
MARY AND MARTHA*

His Nature

The mother's love is like God's love; He loves us not because we are lovable, but because it is His nature to love, and because we are His children.

— EARL RINEY

Breathe Deeply!

Whether you work outside the home or at home—you're busy. When you feel that overwhelming sense of "I don't think I can do one more thing today" taking over—stop! Breathe deeply and remember that God promised He'd never give you more than you can handle. Isn't that good news?

— MICHELLE MEDLOCK ADAMS

An Unfinished Symphony

This life is not all. It is an "unfinished symphony". . .with those who know that they are related to God and have felt "the power of an endless life."

— HENRY WARD BEECHER

Preciously Loved

We are so preciously loved by God that we cannot even comprehend it. No created being can ever know how much and how sweetly and tenderly God loves them.

— St. Julian of Norwich

God Sends Children. . .

God sends children. . .to enlarge our hearts, to make us
unselfish, and full of kindly sympathies and affections;
to give our souls higher aims, to call out all our faculties to
extended enterprise and exertion; to bring round our fireside
bright faces and happy smiles, and loving, tender hearts.

— MARY HOWITT

God's Glory

All God's glory and beauty come from within,
and there He delights to dwell. His visits there
are frequent, His conversation sweet,
His comforts refreshing, His peace
passing all understanding.

— THOMAS À KEMPIS

Walk without Fear

We walk without fear, full of hope and courage
and strength to do His will, waiting for the
endless good which He is always giving as fast
as He can get us to take it in.

— GEORGE MACDONALD

Day 99

God Wants Us to Trust Him

God doesn't want us to know the future; He wants us
to know Him. He wants us to trust Him to guide us
into the future one step at a time.

— STORMIE OMARTIAN

Upon Your Hearts

These commandments that I give you today are to be upon your hearts. Impress them on your children. Talk about them when you sit at home and when you walk along the road, when you lie down and when you get up.

— DEUTERONOMY 6:6–7 NIV

Remember

Mothers. . . Remember, when you rock your babies and sing a lullaby, your arms and voice are God's. When you do load after load of dirty diapers, and then grass-stained play clothes, and finally school clothes smeared with ketchup and chocolate pudding, remember, your hands are God's hands. . . . Through you, He will imprint Himself on your children's hearts.

— ELLYN SANNA

Shine through Me

Dear Lord. . .shine through me, and be so in me
that every soul I come in contact with may feel
Your presence in my soul. . . . Let me thus praise
You in the way You love best, by shining on
those around me.

—JOHN HENRY NEWMAN

A Morning Star

From far beyond our world of trouble and care and change, our Lord shines with undimmed light, a radiant, guiding Star to all who will follow Him—a morning Star, promise of a better day.

— CHARLES E. HURLBURT
AND T. C. HORTON

Meant to Be Immortal

Our Creator would never have made such lovely days,
and have given us the deep hearts to enjoy them, above
and beyond all thought, unless we were meant to be immortal.

— NATHANIEL HAWTHORNE

Life after Lists!

I'm happy to say that there is life after lists. I am a recovering to-do list maker. I've found such freedom in trusting God with my daily activities. Sure, I still have reminder sticky notes scattered around my house, but now I'm not ruled by a list. I've learned there is sweet rest and freedom in trusting God with my day.

— MICHELLE MEDLOCK ADAMS

Let Your
Light Shine

Our gifts and attainments are not only to be
light and warmth in our own dwellings,
but are also to shine through the windows
into the dark night, to guide and cheer
bewildered travelers on the road.

— HENRY WARD BEECHER

A Mother Is a Teacher

For the mother is and must be, whether she knows it or not, the greatest, strongest, and most lasting teacher her children have.

— HANNAH WHITALL SMITH

Spirit of Delight

I love all that thou lovest,
Spirit of Delight!
The fresh Earth in new leaves dressed,
And the starry night;
Autumn evening, and the morn
When the golden mists are born.

— PERCY BYSSHE SHELLEY

I Long For. . .

I long for scenes where man has never trod;
A place where woman never smil'd or wept;
There to abide with my creator, God,
And sleep as I in childhood sweetly slept;
Untroubling and untroubled where I lie;
The grass below—above the vaulted sky.

—JOHN CLARE

Mission Accomplished

One day, we won't have to settle for brief spells of soul satisfaction. We'll spend all eternity singing God praises for the victories He gave us on earth. Our mission accomplished, we'll fill heaven with the rejoicing of satisfied souls.

— TONI SORTOR

I Thank You, God

I thank You, God, for this most amazing day,
for the leaping greenly spirits of trees, and for the
blue dream of sky and for everything which is
natural, which is infinite, which is yes.

— E. E. CUMMINGS

Depending on God

Hope is not a granted wish or a favor performed; no, it is far greater than that. It is a zany, unpredictable dependence on a God who loves to surprise us out of our socks.

— MAX LUCADO

Beauty of Peace

Drop thy still dews of quietness,
Till all our strivings cease;
Take from our souls the strain and stress,
And let our ordered lives confess
The beauty of thy peace.

—JOHN G. WHITTIER

In Faith

No ray of sunshine is ever lost, but the green
which it awakens into existence needs time
to sprout, and it is not always granted for the
sower to see the harvest. All work that is worth
anything is done in faith.

— ALBERT SCHWEITZER

We Thank You, Lord

Lord, behold our family here assembled. We thank
You for this place in which we dwell, for the love
that unites us, for the peace accorded us this day. . .
for the health, the work, the food and the bright
skies that make our lives delightful; for our friends
in all parts of the earth. Amen.

— ROBERT LOUIS STEVENSON

I Can Do All Things

God's Word says that we can do *all* things through Christ who gives us strength. All means all, right! So no matter how you feel today, you can accomplish whatever is on your plate. See, you don't have to *feel* powerful to *be* powerful. The God in you is all-powerful, and He will cause you to triumph.

— MICHELLE MEDLOCK ADAMS

My Crown

My crown is in my heart, not on my head,
Not decked with diamonds
and Indian stones,
Nor to be seen; my crown is called content;
A crown it is that seldom kings enjoy.

— WILLIAM SHAKESPEARE

Rhythms of Life

In waiting we begin to get in touch with the
rhythms of life. . . . They are the rhythms of
God. It is in the everyday and the commonplace
that we learn patience, acceptance,
and contentment.

— RICHARD J. FOSTER

First I'll Be a Mother

Some houses try to hide the fact that
children shelter there.
Ours boasts of it quite openly.
The signs are everywhere.
For smears are on the windows,
little smudges on the doors;
I should apologize, I guess, for toys strewn on the floor.
But I sat down with the children,
and we played and laughed and read.
And if the doorbell doesn't shine,
their eyes will shine instead.
For when at times I'm forced to choose
the one job or the other,
I want to be a housewife—but first I'll be a mother.

— UNKNOWN

To the End

Love never gives up. Love cares more for others than for self. Love doesn't want what it doesn't have. . .doesn't force itself on others, isn't always "me first," doesn't fly off the handle, doesn't keep score of the sins of others. . .puts up with anything, trusts God always, always looks for the best, never looks back, but keeps going to the end.

— 1 CORINTHIANS 13:4–7 MSG

Come Forth as Gold

We will all "come forth as gold" if we understand that God is sovereign and knows what is best, even when we cannot understand what is happening at the time. He asks us to trust Him and to know that He cares for us even when we can't track Him.

— SHIRLEY DOBSON

The Wonder of Living

The wonder of living is held within the beauty of silence, the glory of sunlight, the sweetness of fresh spring air, the quiet strength of earth, and the love that lies at the very root of all things.

— ANONYMOUS

Loving Him

God did not tell us to follow Him because He
needed our help, but because He knew that
loving Him would make us whole.

— IRENAEUS

Heaven

We do not need to search for heaven, over here or over there, in order to find our eternal Father. In fact, we do not even need to speak out loud, for though we speak in the smallest whisper or the most fleeting thought, He is close enough to hear us.

— TERESA OF AVILA

Mother's Knee

There was a place in childhood
that I remember well,
And there a voice of sweetest tone,
bright fairy tales did tell,
And gentle word and fond embrace
were given with joy to me
When I was in the happy place
upon my mother's knee.

— SAMUEL LOVER

Precious Life

Do not let trifles disturb your tranquility of
mind. . . . Life is too precious to be sacrificed for
the nonessential and transient. . . .
Ignore the inconsequential.

— GRENVILLE KLEISER

Play

Many times in our quest to be the perfect mom, we lose sight of the big picture—our children need our love and attention more than anything. For example, stop trying to *plan* the perfect party games and actually *play* some games with your kids today. It's time.

— MICHELLE MEDLOCK ADAMS

Earth Cloaks Your Heaven

Life is so full of meaning and purpose, so full of beauty, beneath its covering, that you will find that earth but cloaks your heaven.

— Fra Giovanni Giocondo

Renewed

By reading the scriptures I am so renewed
that all nature seems renewed around me and
with me. The sky seems to be a pure, a cooler
blue, the trees a deeper green. The whole
world is charged with the glory of God, and I
feel fire and music under my feet.

— THOMAS MERTON

The Soul Is a Temple

The soul is a temple, and God is silently
building it by night and by day. Precious
thoughts are building it, unselfish love is
building it, all-penetrating faith is building it.

— HENRY WARD BEECHER

Day 131

I Wish You...

I wish you love, and strength, and faith, and wisdom,
Goods, gold enough to help some needy one. . . .
And God's sweet peace when every day is done.

— Dorothy Nell McDonald

Just Rest

All people need to get away from everything and everybody on a regular basis for thought, prayer, and just rest. . . . These times of stillness offer me the chance to look within and nurture the real me.

— EMILIE BARNES

Give Me Grace

Oh, God, give me grace for this day.
Not for a lifetime, nor for next week,
nor for tomorrow, just for this day.

— MARJORIE HOLMES

Hints of Hereafter

Human love and the delights of friendship,
out of which are built the memories that
endure, are also to be treasured up as hints of
what shall be hereafter.

— BEDE JARRETT

Nothing Lacks Attention

Not even the tiny dewdrops lack the attention of the
Lover of all. Shall I then think of any detail of my
earthly life, even so little a thing as the minute of
one of my hours, as without meaning?

— Elisabeth Elliot

The Greatest Glow

When we recall the past, we usually find that it is the simplest things—not the great occasions—that in retrospect give off the greatest glow of happiness.

—Bob Hope

Just as You Are

Comparing yourself with others is never a good thing, and it's not a God thing, either. God isn't concerned with whether or not your belly is as trim as it was before childbirth. He's concerned with the condition of your heart. Find your identity in Him. He loves you just the way you are.

—— MICHELLE MEDLOCK ADAMS

No One Else

Your identity is the result of neither coincidence nor accident. You are who you are because of God's loving design. He wanted you to be *you*, and no one else.

— DARLENE SALA

Choice

Happiness in the older years of life, like happiness
in every year of life, is a matter of choice——
your choice for yourself.

— HAROLD AZINE

Embraced. . .

"You're blessed when you're at the end of your rope.
With less of you there is more of God and his rule. You're
blessed when you feel you've lost what is most dear to you.
Only then can you be embraced by the One most dear to you."

— MATTHEW 5:3–4 MSG

Worth Living For

Children make love stronger, days shorter,
nights longer, bankrolls smaller,
homes happier, clothes shabbier, the past
forgotten, and the future worth living for.

— ANONYMOUS

The Perfect Picture

The painter has with his brush transferred the landscape to the canvas with such fidelity that the trees and grasses seem almost real; he has made even the face of a maiden seem instinct with life, but there is one picture so beautiful that no painter has ever been able perfectly to reproduce it, and that is the picture of the mother holding in her arms her babe.

— WILLIAM JENNINGS BRYAN

Happy Chance

We are not the same persons this year as last; nor are
those we love. It is a happy chance if we, changing,
continue to love as a changed person.

— W. SOMERSET MAUGHAM

Day by Day

I love to think that God appoints
my portion day by day;
Events of life are in His hand,
and I would only say,
Appoint them in Thine own good time,
and in Thine own best way.

— A. L. WARING

Your Best Harvest

Your best harvest may be the pleasure you get
from working with family and friends.
There's never a shortage of things to do, and
no limit to the lessons that can be learned.

—— STEVEN WILLSON

We Travel with God

It is God to whom and with whom we travel;
and while He is the End of our journey,
He is also at every stopping place.

— ELISABETH ELLIOT

Day 147

Dreams Are Renewable

No matter what your age or your condition,
your dreams are renewable. Whether you're 5 or 105,
you have a lifetime ahead of you!

— Unknown

He Is the Way!

Getting lost used to really frustrate and frighten me.
Now, I consider it more of a fun adventure. I find that
something good usually comes from it. You see, it's all in
the perspective. Life is the same way. There's no sense
worrying your way through each day. If we know Jesus as
our Lord and Savior, we're on the right road because
He is the Way!

— MICHELLE MEDLOCK ADAMS

Our Father's Business

God is a kind Father. He sets us all in the places where He wishes us to be employed; and that employment is truly "our Father's business." He chooses work for every creature. . . . He gives us always strength enough, and sense enough, for what He wants us to do.

—JOHN RUSKIN

Holy Disruption

Though I have never been a fan of chaos,
as I get a little older (and hopefully a little
wiser, too), I'm trying to let my kids be the holy
disruption God wants them to be in my life.

— DENA DYER

Day 151

The Best Things

The best things are nearest: breath in the nostrils,
light in your eyes, flowers at your feet, duties at
your hand, the path of God just before you.

— ROBERT LOUIS STEVENSON

God Takes Pleasure in You

Think of it—not one whorled finger exactly like another!
If God should take such delight in designing fingertips, think
how much pleasure the unfurling of your life must give Him.

— LUCIE CHRISTOPHER

Rubbing Elbows with Happiness

Sometimes our thoughts turn back toward a corner in a forest, or the end of a bank, or an orchard powdered with flowers, seen but a single time. . .yet remaining in our hearts. . . a feeling we have just rubbed elbows with happiness.

— GUY DE MAUPASSANT

A Pulse, a Sequence, a Journey

The seasons remind me that I play one small part in a bigger picture—that there is a pulse, a sequence, a journey set into motion by the very hand of God Himself.

— KAREN SCALF LINAMEN

God Grant You Many Years

God grant you many and happy years,
Till, when the last has crowned you,
The dawn of endless days appears,
And heaven is shining around you.

— OLIVER WENDELL HOLMES

Wonder of the World

I still find each day too short for all the thoughts I want to think, all the walks I want to take, all the books I want to read, and all the friends I want to see. The longer I live, the more my mind dwells upon the beauty and the wonder of the world.

—JOHN BURROUGHS

Memory and Hope

A strange thing is memory, and hope; one looks backward, and the other forward; one is of today, the other of tomorrow. Memory is history recorded in our brain, memory is a painter, it paints pictures of the past and of the day.

—— GRANDMA MOSES

Make Me a Blessing

Earlier today, I was so discouraged.
As a mother, as a Christian, I felt like a failure.
Life weighed me down until I couldn't see
anything You had accomplished for me. Then
I thought of the song "Count Your Blessings."
When I started the list, I couldn't stop finding
ways You had fulfilled Your promises to me.
The miracle of having children is one of those
blessings, Lord. Make me a blessing
to my children.

— FROM *PRAYERS AND PROMISES FOR MOTHERS*

Teach and Pray

I realize that I can't pick my children's friends,
and I know that I can't protect them from the hurt
that comes from broken friendships and disloyalty.
But, there are two things I can do—I can teach
them about Jesus, and I can pray that the Lord
sends them godly friends. You can do the same for
your kids. You can start today.

— MICHELLE MEDLOCK ADAMS

Transformed

Don't copy the behavior and customs of this world, but let
God transform you into a new person by changing the way
you think. Then you will learn to know God's will for you,
which is good and pleasing and perfect.

— Romans 12:2 NLT

Thank You, God, for Mother

Thank You, God, for Mother.
She brings us all such joy,
And thank You for the love
she gives to every girl and boy.
Dear God, when I am bigger, help me, too, to see,
Life as a gift, to share in love,
And like my Mother be.

— ANONYMOUS

In the Present Moment

The art of life is to live in the present moment,
and to make that moment as perfect as we can by
the realization that we are the instruments and
expression of God Himself.

—EMMET FOX

Day 163

A Beacon

A mother's happiness is like a beacon, lighting up the future but reflected also on the past in the guise of fond memories.

— HONORÉ DE BALZAC

Silence

We need to find God, and He cannot be found in noise
and restlessness. God is the friend of silence.
See how nature—trees, flowers, grass—grows in silence;
see the stars, the moon and the sun, how they move in
silence. . . . We need silence to be able to touch souls.

— MOTHER TERESA

Extending Grace

Let's not judge one another for the decisions
we make about working or staying at home,
nursing or bottle-feeding,
and homeschooling versus public schooling.
Instead, I pray that we moms will give
ourselves, and each other, grace.

— DENA DYER

A Balanced Life

Be aware of wonder. Live a balanced life—learn
some and think some and draw and paint and sing
and dance and play and work every day some.

—Robert Fulghum

Golden Moments

The golden moments in the stream of life rush past
us, and we see nothing but sand; the angels come to
visit us, and we only know them when they are gone.

— GEORGE ELIOT

Like a River

Time is a sort of river of passing events, and strong is its
current; no sooner is a thing brought to sight than it is
swept by and another takes its place, and this, too,
will be swept away.

— Marcus Aurelius

Bring Your Troubles to God

We sometimes fear to bring our troubles to God, because they must seem small to Him who sitteth on the circle of the earth. But if they are large enough to vex and endanger our welfare, they are large enough to touch His heart of love.

— R. A. TORREY

Simple Wonders

A fiery sunset, tiny pansies by the wayside, the sound of raindrops tapping on the roof— what an extraordinary delight to share simple wonders with our children! With wide eyes and full hearts, we may come to cherish what others have missed.

— ANONYMOUS

Tomorrow

Do not look forward to what may happen
tomorrow; the same everlasting Father who cares
for you today will take care of you tomorrow and
every day. Either He will shield you from suffering,
or He will give you unfailing strength to bear it.
Be at peace then, and put aside all anxious
thoughts and imaginations.

— ST. FRANCIS DE SALES

Thankful for His Love

The Lord knew what He was doing when He put our families together. He knew that our kids would fight, and He knew they'd need each other. And here's another comforting thought—God desires for them to be buddies, too. So, the next time your children are bickering, don't get discouraged. Just thank the Lord for His love in your home.

— MICHELLE MEDLOCK ADAMS

A Childlike Appetite

Whether sixty or sixteen, there is in every human being's heart the love of wonder; the sweet amazement at the stars and starlike things, the undaunted challenge of events, the unfailing childlike appetite for what-next, and the joy of the game of living.

— SAMUEL ULLMAN

Day 174

The Secret of a Good Memory

The secret of a good memory is attention,
and attention to a subject depends upon our
interest in it. We rarely forget that which has
made a deep impression on our minds.

— TRYON EDWARDS

Every Experience

Every experience God gives us, every person He puts in our lives, is the perfect preparation for the future that only He can see.

— CORRIE TEN BOOM

Incessant Prayer

Whether words are uttered or not, lifting the heart to God while one is occupied with miscellaneous duties is the vital thing. [Incessant prayer is] the only way to cultivate a joyful attitude in times of trial.

— ROBERT L. THOMAS

I Am Only One

I am only one, but I am one. I cannot do everything, but I can do something. And that which I can do, by the grace of God, I will do.

— DWIGHT L. MOODY

A Perfect Day

For memory has painted this perfect day
With colors that never fade,
And we find at the end of a perfect day
The soul of a friend we've made.

— CARRIE JACOBS BOND

A Net

Memory is a net: one that finds it full of fish when
he takes it from the brook, but a dozen miles of
water have run through it without sticking.

— OLIVER WENDELL HOLMES

To Little Children

At that time Jesus, full of joy through the Holy Spirit, said, "I praise you, Father, Lord of heaven and earth, because you have hidden these things from the wise and learned, and revealed them to little children. Yes, Father, for this was your good pleasure."

— LUKE 10:21 NIV

In Quietness

Learn but in quietness and stillness to retire to the Lord, and wait upon Him; in whom thou shall feel peace and joy, in the midst of thy trouble from the cruel and vexatious spirit of this world. So wait to know thy work and service to the Lord every day, in thy place and station; and the Lord make thee faithful therein, and thou wilt want neither help, support, nor comfort.

— ISAAC PENINGTON

My First Great Love

[My mother] is my first, great love.
She was a wonderful, rare woman as strong
and steadfast and generous as the sun. She
could be as kind and gentle as warm rain, and
as steadfast as the irreducible earth beneath us.

— D. H. LAWRENCE

Place Your Hand in God's

Go out into the darkness and put your hand into the Hand of God. That shall be to you better light and safer than a known way.

— MINNIE LOUISE HASKINS

Never-Ending Love

A mother has ears that truly listen,
arms that always hold.
She has a love that's never-ending
and a heart made of purest gold.

— ANONYMOUS

You

Christ has no body now on earth but yours;
yours are the only hands with which He can
do His work, yours are the only feet with
which He can go about the world, yours are
the only eyes through which His compassion
can shine forth upon a troubled world.
Christ has no body on earth now but you.

— St. Teresa of Avila

God Has You Covered

While there's no magic "worrywart potion" on the market, you have easy access to one that you might not have considered—God's Word! It will obliterate worry if you'll only believe it. God's got you covered. Worry never changed anything, but God's Word always does.

— MICHELLE MEDLOCK ADAMS

Heavenly Paradise

There is a garden in her face
Where roses and white lilies grow;
A heavenly paradise is that place
Wherein all pleasant fruits do flow.

— THOMAS CAMPION

Beautiful World

Great wide, beautiful, wonderful world,
With the wonderful waters round you curled,
And the wonderful grass upon your breast,
World, you are beautifully dressed.

— WILLIAM BRIGHTLY RANDS

Springtime in My Soul

There is springtime in my soul today,
For, when the Lord is near,
The dove of peace sings in my heart,
The flowers of grace appear.

— ELIZA HEWITT

The Holy

Every encounter, every incident during the day is grist for the mill of the ongoing God-human communication. No activity is too small or too unimportant to mediate the holy.

— NORVENE VEST

Humble Tasks

I long to accomplish great and noble tasks, but it is my chief duty to accomplish humble tasks as though they were great and noble. The world is moved along not only by the mighty shoves of its heroes, but also by the aggregate of the tiny pushes of each honest worker.

— HELEN KELLER

I Thank You

For childhood's golden memories
For happy bygone years
The comfort of your presence
In days of joy or tears
For all your love upon life's way—
I thank you from my heart this day.

—ANONYMOUS

Guide Me, O Lord

Guide me, O Lord, in all the changes and varieties of the world; that in all things that shall happen I may have an evenness and tranquility of spirit; that my soul may be wholly resigned to Thy divine will and pleasure, never murmuring at Thy gentle chastisements and fatherly correction. Amen.

— JEREMY TAYLOR

Memories

When we start to count flowers,
we cease to count weeds;
When we start to count blessings,
we cease to count needs;
When we start to count laughter,
we cease to count tears;
When we start to count memories,
we cease to count years.

—Anonymous

Rest and Delight

Bundle me up in an old, worn quilt with hand-sewn
stitches and soft cotton batting—place a book upon
my lap, a cup of tea in my hand, a light by my side,
and leave me in a world of rest and delight.

— ANONYMOUS

Lasting Peace

Lasting peace of mind is impossible apart from peace with God: yet enduring peace with God comes only when a man is ready to surrender of his own peace of mind.

— A. ROY ECKARDT

Search for God

The Bible nowhere calls upon men to go out
in search of peace of mind. It does call upon
men to go out in search of God and
the things of God.

— ABBA SILVER

Inner Simplicity

Attaining inner simplicity is learning to live happily in the present moment. Keep in mind that life is a continuous succession of present moments.

— ELAINE ST. JAMES

Speak, Lord

Speak, Lord, for Thy servant heareth,
  speak peace to my anxious soul,
And help me to feel that all my ways
  are under Thy wise control;
That He who cares for the lily,
  and heeds the sparrows' fall,
Shall tenderly lead His loving child:
  for He made and loveth all.

— UNKNOWN

With Your Whole Heart

GOD, your God, will cut away the thick calluses on your
heart and your children's hearts, freeing you to love
GOD, your God, with your whole heart and soul and live,
really live. . . . And you will make a new start, listening
obediently to GOD, keeping all his commandments that
I'm commanding you today. GOD, your God, will outdo
himself in making things go well for you.

— DEUTERONOMY 30:6–9 MSG

Good Memories

There is nothing higher and stronger and more wholesome and useful for life in later years than some good memory, especially a memory connected with childhood, with home. If we carry many such memories with us into life, we are safe to the end of our days, and if we have only one good memory left in our hearts, even that may sometime be the means of saving us.

— FYODOR DOSTOEVSKY

God's Hand

I'm not sure why I neglect to reach for God's
hand when I'm crossing the busy streets of life.
I guess. . .I think I'm mature enough to handle it
on my own. I'm so thankful that we have a loving
heavenly Father who reaches down to take our
hands when we need Him the most.

— MICHELLE MEDLOCK ADAMS

True Nature of Things

For in the true nature of things, if we will rightly consider, every green tree is far more glorious than if it were made of gold and silver.

— MARTIN LUTHER

In the Forest

In the forest we can rise above our worldly care;
In the forest we may find tranquility and share
The silence and the secret strength
of great and ancient trees—
Sturdy oaks and silver birches,
laughing in the breeze.

— PATIENCE STRONG

Gentle Words

A gentle word, like summer rain,
May soothe some heart and banish pain.
What joy or sadness often springs
From just the simple little things!

— WILLA HOEY

Partner with God

To be a mother is a woman's greatest vocation
in life. She is a partner with God.

— SPENCER W. KIMBALL

Day 207

Where There Is God

Where there is faith, there is love.
Where there is love, there is peace.
Where there is peace, there is God.
Where there is God, there is no need.

— ANONYMOUS

A Voice of Love

There is a voice, "a still, small voice" of love,
Heard from above;
But not amidst the din of earthly sounds,
Which here confounds;
By those withdrawn apart it best is heard,
And peace, sweet peace, breathes in each gentle word.

—— UNKNOWN

Small Things

Is it so small a thing to have enjoyed the sun,
to have lived light in the spring, to have loved,
to have thought, to have done?

— MATTHEW ARNOLD

Unending Praise

May your life become one of glad and unending
praise to the Lord as you journey through this
world, and in the world that is to come!

— TERESA OF AVILA

A Portrait

A man walks through life painting a portrait,
not of what he would have done, could have done,
or should have done, but of what he did.

— ANONYMOUS

Smell the Roses

You're only here for a short visit. Don't hurry, don't worry.
And be sure to smell the flowers along the way.

—— WALTER HAGEN

Your Travel Bag

Own only what you can carry with you;
know language, know countries, know people.
Let your memory be your travel bag.

— ALEXANDER SOLZHENITSYN

Day 214

Hoped For

Do not spoil what you have by desiring which
you have not; but remember that what you
have now was once among the things
you only hoped for.

— EPICURUS

Every Minute

Happiness cannot be traveled to, owned, earned,
worn, or consumed. Happiness is the spiritual
experience of living every minute with love,
grace, and gratitude.

— DENIS WAITLEY

Make Me Teachable

Quiet, Lord, my froward heart;
Make me teachable and mild,
Upright, simple, free from art,
Make me as a weaned child:
From distrust and envy free,
Pleas'd with all that pleases Thee.

— JOHN NEWTON

Nothing but the Best

The mother loves her child most divinely, not when she surrounds him with comfort and anticipates his wants, but when she resolutely holds him to the highest standards and is content with nothing less than his best.

— HAMILTON WRIGHT MABIE

Day 218

God's Word

Daily, I ask God to help me live out my faith.
If my life is an open book before my [children],
I want to make sure it's full of God's Word.
How about you? Encourage your kids to read
God's Word and then live your life according to
His Word. That's a one-two punch
against the devil!

— MICHELLE MEDLOCK ADAMS

The Hand that Rocks the Cradle

They say that man is mighty,
He governs land and sea;
He wields a mighty scepter
O'er lesser powers that be;
And the hand that rocks the cradle
Is the hand that rules the world.

—— WILLIAM ROSS WALLACE

Inward Treasures

I long to put the experience of fifty years at once into your
young lives, to give you at once the key of that treasure
chamber every gem of which has cost me tears and
struggles and prayers, but you must work for these
inward treasures yourself.

—HARRIET BEECHER STOWE

Praise God

Praise be to the God and Father of our Lord Jesus Christ! In his great mercy he has given us new birth into a living hope through the resurrection of Jesus Christ from the dead, and into an inheritance that can never perish, spoil or fade— kept in heaven for you, who through faith are shielded by God's power.

— 1 PETER 1:3–5 NIV

The Big Picture

Don't let the tedium of each day's chores and
responsibilities wear you down. . . . Keep your
eyes on the big picture. Focus on why you do
what you do and who will benefit from your
work, including those you don't know and may
never meet. You may not have all the answers
to the question "Why am I here?" but you can
rest assured that the Lord does!

— FROM *QUIET MOMENTS
WITH GOD FOR MOTHERS*

The Very First Smile

A mother once asked a clergyman when she should
begin the education of her child. . . "Madam," was
the reply. . . "From the very first smile that gleams
over an infant's cheek, your opportunity begins."

— RICHARD WHATELY

The Real Rock

We want to make sure that our children don't think of God
as a passing fad but as a steadfast part of their lives.
To ensure that, we can feed them God's Word.
We can also let our children see us loving God and His
Word. Most importantly, we can pray that our kids will
always love God—the real Rock.

— MICHELLE MEDLOCK ADAMS

The Best Education

You are told a lot about your education, but some beautiful, sacred memory, preserved since childhood, is perhaps the best education of all. If a man carries many such memories into life with him, he is saved for the rest of his days.

— FYODOR DOSTOEVSKY

Our Lives Are Blest

It is in loving, not in being loved,
The heart finds its quest;
It is in giving, not in getting,
Our lives are blest.

— UNKNOWN

Day 227

How Far Will You Go?

How far you go in life depends on your being
tender with the young, compassionate with the
aged, sympathetic with the striving, and tolerant of
the weak and the strong. Because someday in life,
you will have been all of these.

— GEORGE WASHINGTON CARVER

On the Run

Half the joy of life is in little things taken on the run.
Let us run if we must. . .but let us keep our hearts young and
our eyes open that nothing worth our while shall escape us.

— CHARLES VICTOR CHERBULIEZ

The Lord's Day

Father, give me the grace today to take time.
Time to be with You. Time to be with others.
Time to enjoy the life You have given me.
Help me remember that today is the day You
have made. May I rejoice and be glad in it!
Amen.

— LUCI SWINDOLL

Mother Dear

Once upon a memory
Someone wiped away a tear
Held me close and loved me,
Thank you, Mother dear.

— UNKNOWN

A Softer Light

There is a religion in all deep love, but the love of
a mother is the veil of a softer light between the
heart and the heavenly Father.

— Samuel Taylor Coleridge

Listen!

It is a beauteous evening, calm and free,
The holy time is quiet as a Nun
Breathless with adoration; the broad sun
Is sinking down in its tranquility;
The gentleness of heaven broods o'er the Sea;
Listen! the mighty Being is awake,
And doth with his eternal motion make
A sound like thunder—everlastingly.

— WILLIAM WORDSWORTH

Devotion

My sainted mother taught me a devotion to
God and a love to country which have ever
sustained me in my many lonely and bitter
moments of decision in distant and hostile
lands. To her, I yield anew a son's
reverent devotion.

— GENERAL DOUGLAS MACARTHUR

Her Footsteps

There is no velvet so soft as a mother's lap,
no rose as lovely as her smile, no path so
flowery as that imprinted with her footsteps.

— ARCHIBALD THOMPSON

The Hand of a Mother

Education is the mental railway, beginning at birth and running on to eternity. No hand can lay it in the right direction but the hand of a mother.

— Mrs. H. O. Ward

Little Things

Life is not made up of great sacrifices and duties but of little things: in which smiles and kindness given habitually are what win and preserve the heart and secure comfort.

— SIR HUMPHREY DAVY

The Child's Heart

Is the world all grown up? Is childhood dead?
Or is there not in the bosom of the wisest and
the best, some of the child's heart left?

— CHARLES LAMB

Thank God for Everything

Make it a rule to yourself to thank and praise God for everything that happens to you. For it is certain that whatever seeming calamity happens to you, if you thank and praise God for it, you turn it into a blessing. Could you, therefore, work miracles, you could not do more for yourself than by this thankful spirit; for it heals with a word speaking and turns all that it touches into happiness.

— WILLIAM LAW

Day 239

A Mother. . .

A mother is a person who, seeing there are
only four pieces of pie for five people, promptly
announces she never did care for pie.

— TENNEVA JORDAN

Sacrifice

Think of the sacrifice your mother had to make in order
that you might live. Think of the sacrifice God had to
make that you and your mother might live.

— UNKNOWN

So that We Might Be Rich

For you know the grace of our Lord Jesus Christ, that though he was rich, yet for your sakes he became poor, so that you through his poverty might become rich.

—2 CORINTHIANS 8:9 NIV

Let Them Learn

If you would have your children to walk
honorable through the world, you must not
attempt to clear the stones from their path,
but teach them to walk firmly over them—not to
insist on leading them by the hand, but let them
learn to go alone.

— ANNE BRONTË

Words of Praise

Words of praise, indeed, are almost as necessary to warm a child into a genial life as acts of kindness and affection. Judicious praise is to children what the sun is to flowers.

— CHRISTIAN NESTELL BOVEE

Stop, Pause, and Praise

Daily aggravations will be a part of life until we get to
heaven. We just have to learn how to deal with them.
Here's the plan: Today if something goes wrong—stop,
pause, and praise. Praise God *in spite* of the aggravation.
Before long the "stop, pause, and praise" practice will
become a habit, the kind of habit worth forming!

— MICHELLE MEDLOCK ADAMS

True Beauty

People are like stained-glass windows.
They sparkle and shine when the sun is out,
but when the darkness sets in, their true beauty
is revealed only if there is light from within.

—— Elisabeth Kübler-Ross

Sea of Glass

Christ's life outwardly was one of the most
troubled lives that was ever lived; tempest
and tumult, tumult and tempest, the waves
breaking over it all the time. . . . But the inner
life was a sea of glass. The great calm was
always there.

— HENRY DRUMMOND

No Worries!

As long as we're on this earth, there will be
trouble. God tells us that in His Word, but He also
tells us not to fret over it. That means it's actually
possible to encounter stress and problems and still
have no worries. The next time you encounter
trouble, say, "No worries!" and mean it!

— MICHELLE MEDLOCK ADAMS

All Are Known

Nay, all by Thee is ordered, chosen, planned;
Each drop that fills my daily cup Thy hand
Prescribes, for ills none else can understand:
All, all are known to Thee.

— ADELAIDE LEAPER NEWTON

Yield Thyself

Thine own self-will and anxiety, thy hurry and labor, disturb thy peace, and prevent Me from working in thee. Look at the little flowers, in the serene summer days; they quietly open their petals, and the sun shines into them with his gentle influences. So will I do for thee, if thou wilt yield thyself to Me.

— GERHARD TERSTEEGEN

You Made My Life Complete

Mom, your love and direction have helped me
more than you'll ever know. Without your love,
my life would not have been complete because
you taught me the meaning of love.
God bless you and keep you safe always.

— ANONYMOUS

Inexpressible Joy

What inexpressible joy for me, to look up through the apple blossoms and the fluttering leaves, and to see God's love there; to listen to the thrush that has built his nest among them, and to feel God's love, who cares for the birds, in every note that swells his little throat; to look beyond to the bright blue depths of the sky, and feel they are a canopy of blessing—the roof of the house of my Father. . . .

— ELIZABETH RUNDELL CHARLES

Gems and Pearls

Dissect a mother's heart and see the properties it doth
contain—what pearls of love, what gems of hope.
A mother's heart beats not in vain.

— CALEB DUNN

Second to God

The woman who creates and sustains a
home, and under whose hands children grow
up to be strong and pure men and women is
a creator second only to God.

— HELEN HUNT JACKSON

Glad Hearts

Your greatest pleasure is that which rebounds
from hearts that you have made glad.

— HENRY WARD BEECHER

The Voice of God

If ye keep watch over your hearts, and listen for the voice of God, and learn of Him, in one short hour ye can learn more from Him than ye could learn from man in a thousand years.

——JOHANNES TAULER

Heavenly Fire

There is in every true woman's heart a spark of heavenly
fire, which lies dormant in the broad daylight of prosperity,
but which kindles up and beams and blazes in the dark
hour of adversity.

— WASHINGTON IRVING

The Rewind Button!

Of course you always love your kids. But, if you're like me, there are days when you don't particularly love everything about them. At the end of those days I want to hit the rewind button and start the day over again, but it's impossible. God does have a rewind button, though! He lets us start over every time we fail.

— MICHELLE MEDLOCK ADAMS

The Greater the Pressure

J. Hudson Taylor, that great pioneer missionary to China, used to say we should not mind how great the pressure is—only where the pressure lies. If we make sure it never comes between us and our Lord, then the greater the pressure, the more it presses us to Him.

— RUTH BELL GRAHAM

Indispensable

Everyone has a unique role to fill in the world and is
important in some respect. Everyone, including and
perhaps especially you, is indispensable.

— NATHANIEL HAWTHORNE

Make Me a Saint

Lord of all pots and pans and things,
Since I've no time to be
A saint by doing lovely things. . .
Make me a saint by getting meals
And washing up the plates. . . .
Accept this service that I do—
I do it unto Thee.

— UNKNOWN

His Power Works within Us

Now to him who is able to do immeasurably more than all we ask or imagine, according to his power that is at work within us, to him be glory in the church and in Christ Jesus throughout all generations, for ever and ever! Amen.

— EPHESIANS 3:20–21 NIV

Resting on the Rock

I hold not the Rock, but the Rock holds me,
The Rock holds me. . .
I rest on the Rock, and the Rock holds me,
Resting on the Rock of God.

— Mrs. C. Rice

Day 263

Minute Fractions

The happiness of life is made up of minute fractions—
the little soon forgotten charities of a kiss or smile,
a kind look, a heartfelt compliment, and the countless
infinitesimal of pleasurable and genial feeling.

— SAMUEL TAYLOR COLERIDGE

Love Might Rule

Say to mothers what a holy charge is theirs.
With what a kingly power their love might rule
the fountains of the newborn mind.

— LYDIA H. SIGOURNEY

The Golden Link

A mother's love is indeed the golden link that
binds youth to age; and he is still but a child
who can yet recall, with a softened heart,
the fond devotion, or the gentle chidings,
of the best friend that God ever gives us.

— CHRISTIAN NESTELL BOVEE

The Best Fortune

Give me the life of the boy whose mother is nurse, seamstress, washerwoman, cook, teacher, angel, and saint, all in one, and whose father is guide, exemplar, and friend. No servants to come between. These are the boys who are born to the best fortune.

— ANDREW CARNEGIE

Permission to Rest

The age we live in has been described as
the age of the to-do list that can't be done.
Facing overwhelming demands, we find it hard to
give ourselves permission to rest or take a break.
But the rewards—renewed perspective,
clearer insight, physical energy, and spiritual
preparedness—are well worth it.

— FROM *QUIET MOMENTS*
WITH GOD FOR MOTHERS

Our Daily Bread

He only is the Maker of all things near and far;
He paints the wayside flower,
He lights the evening star;
The wind and waves obey Him,
by Him the birds are fed;
Much more to us, His children,
He gives our daily bread.

— MATTHIAS CLAUDIUS

Language of the Heart

Occasionally in life there are those moments of unutterable fulfillment which cannot be completely explained by those symbols called words. Their meanings can only be articulated by the inaudible language of the heart.

— MARTIN LUTHER KING JR.

Kind Words

Kind words produce their own image in
men's souls; and a beautiful image it is.
They soothe and quiet and comfort the hearer.
. . . We have not yet begun to use kind words in
such abundance as they ought to be used.

— BLAISE PASCAL

Lovebeam

Just as there comes a warm sunbeam into every
cottage window, so comes a lovebeam of God's care
and pity for every separate need.

— NATHANIEL HAWTHORNE

Your Child

Lord, I am Your child, and You delight in me whenever I fall. You pick me up, give me a hug, and encourage me to try again. Thank You for rejoicing over me.

— RACHEL QUILLIN AND
NANCY J. FARRIER

A Rare Book

A child is a rare book of which but only one copy is made.

— UNKNOWN

Islands of Stillness

Teach me the art of creating islands of stillness,
in which I can absorb the beauty of everyday
things: clouds, trees, a snatch of music. . .

— MARION STROUD

Unique Gifts

I don't have to exaggerate my strengths or claim gifts that I don't have. I can count on others who have the gifts I don't. But I should not undervalue myself, because my true self-esteem comes from knowing that my unique gifts are as necessary to the body of Christ as anyone else's.

— Lyn Klug

A Sacred Beauty

She wore age so gracefully, so carelessly, that there was a sacred beauty about her faded cheek more lovely and lovable than all the bloom of her youth.

— DINAH MARIA MULOCK

Example

Sometimes I wonder—what kind of example am I leaving my children? What will they write on my tombstone or say about me after I'm gone? . . . Hopefully my epitaph will read something like this: "She hated folding laundry but liked to fold us in her arms."

—— DENA DYER

Remember Childhood

Let me play in the sunshine;
Let me sing for joy;
Let me grow in the light;
Let me splash in the rain,
And remember the days of my childhood forever.

— UNKNOWN

Your Best and Worst Days

Your worst days are never so bad that you are beyond the reach of God's grace. And your best days are never so good that you are beyond the need of God's grace.

—JERRY BRIDGES

Day 280

Lord, Rejuvenate My Soul

Lord, I'm overwhelmed. . . . I often lose sight of You. Please rejuvenate my soul and help me look to You for strength and comfort when I need it most. Remind me that I can't control everything and that it's okay I'm not perfect. Amen.

— FROM *IN THE KITCHEN WITH MARY AND MARTHA: ONE-DISH WONDERS*

God Lifts Us Up

Humble yourselves therefore under the mighty
hand of God, so that he may exalt you in due
time. Cast all your anxiety on him,
because he cares for you.

— 1 PETER 5:6–7 NRSV

His All

An infinite God can give all of Himself to each of
His children. He does not distribute Himself that
each may have a part, but to each one He gives
all of Himself as fully as if there were no others.

— A. W. TOZER

The Perfect Gift

We have a suggestion for the perfect gift for
your child. It is not easy to find, and it is terribly
expensive, but we guarantee that it will last a
lifetime, and it will be your child's favorite.
We're talking about your *time*.

— BRUCE BICKEL AND STAN JANTZ

HELP!

A prayer to be said when the world has gotten you down
and you feel rotten, and you're too doggone tired to pray,
and you're in a big hurry, and besides, you're mad at
everybody: HELP.

— CHARLES SWINDOLL

If I Can...

If I can stop one Heart from breaking
I shall not live in vain
If I can ease one Life the Aching
or cool one Pain
Or help one fainting Robin
Unto his Nest again
I shall not live in Vain.

— EMILY DICKINSON

Energy

Direct your time and energy into worry,
and you will be deficient in things like singing with
grace in your heart, praying with thanksgiving,
listening to a child's account of his school day,
inviting a lonely person to supper, sitting down to
talk unhurriedly with wife or husband,
writing a note to someone who needs it.

— ELISABETH ELLIOT

Inborn Sense of Wonder

If a child is to keep alive his inborn sense of wonder,
he needs the companionship of at least one adult
who can share it, rediscovering with him the joy,
excitement, and mystery of the world we live in.

— RACHEL CARSON

Worth It All

D'you call life a bad job? Never! We've had our ups and
downs, we've had our struggles, we've always been poor,
but it's been worth it, aye, worth it a hundred times,
I say, when I look round at my children.

— W. SOMERSET MAUGHAM

A Miracle

This is the miracle that happens every time to those who really love; the more they give, the more they possess of that precious nourishing love from which flowers and children have their strength.

— RAINER MARIA RILKE

My Heart Is at Rest

When the voices of children
Are heard on the green
And laughing is heard on the hill,
My heart is at rest within my breast
And everything else is still.

— WILLIAM BLAKE

Enjoy Today

If you can eat today, enjoy the sunshine today, mix good cheer with friends today, enjoy it and bless God for it.

—HENRY WARD BEECHER

Lessons to Learn

Take advantage of the natural lull after hard times, when you're pulling together the pieces to sort through the events and ferret out the lessons.

—JEAN FLEMING

Building Patience

Patience can't be acquired overnight. It is just like building up a muscle. Every day you need to work on it.

— EKNATH EASWARAN

Free as Birds

In almost everything that touches our everyday life on earth, God is pleased when we're pleased. He wills that we be as free as birds to soar and sing our Maker's praise without anxiety.

— A. W. TOZER

Learn to Sing

I had eight birds hatcht in one nest,
Four Cocks were there, and Hens the rest.
I nurst them up with pain and care,
No cost nor labour did I spare
Till at last they felt their wing,
Mounted the Trees and learned to sing.

—Anne Bradstreet

One Perfect Thing

Without God's superintendence, our lives would be so complicated and we would be going in so many different directions that we could not function. He has one perfect thing He wants each of us doing at any given time.

—— JO BERRY

Great Gifts

For blessings of the fruitful season,
For work and rest, for friends and home,
For the great gifts of thought and reason—
To praise and bless Thee, Lord, we come.

— ELIZA SCUDDER

Complete Love

Grace means God accepts me just as I am.
He does not require or insist that I measure up to
someone else's standard of performance.
He loves me completely, thoroughly, and
perfectly. There's nothing I can do to add to or
detract from that love.

— MARY GRAHAM

Thank You, God

Thank You, God, for the beauty
Around me everywhere,
The gentle rain, and glistening dew,
The sunshine and the air.

— HELEN STEINER RICE

Quiet My Spirit, Lord

O Lord, today is a hard one. I feel like the weight of the
world is pressing on me, and I'm not handling it well at all.
The kids are fighting. The neighbor wants to talk.
I didn't have a chance to have much of a quiet time with
You. I feel so weak and helpless. Quiet my spirit, Lord.
Let me close my eyes for a moment and experience Your
touch. My strength comes from You.

—— FROM *PRAYERS AND
PROMISES FOR MOTHERS*

From Above

Every good and perfect gift is from above,
coming down from the Father of the heavenly
lights, who does not change like shifting
shadows. He chose to give us birth through
the word of truth, that we might be a kind of
firstfruits of all he created.

— JAMES 1:17–18 NIV

Everything!

God knows everything about us. And He cares
about everything. Moreover, He can manage
every situation. And He loves us! Surely this is
enough to open the wellsprings of joy. . . .
And joy is always a source of strength.

— HANNAH WHITALL SMITH

What a Friend We Have in Jesus

What a friend we have in Jesus,
All our sins and griefs to bear!
What a privilege to carry
Everything to God in prayer!
O what peace we often forfeit,
O what needless pain we bear,
All because we do not carry
Everything to God in prayer.

— JOSEPH M. SCRIVEN

Nature

I love snow and all the forms
Of the radiant frost;
I love waves, and winds, and storms,
Everything almost
Which is Nature's, and may be
Untainted by man's misery.

—— PERCY BYSSHE SHELLEY

Affections

There is an enduring tenderness in the love
of a mother to a child that transcends all
other affections of the heart.

— WASHINGTON IRVING

A Daily Reminder

Make a list of all the things for which you're
thankful. Write it on pretty stationery and
display it on the refrigerator where you'll see
it often—a daily reminder of everything that's
good in your life.

— FROM *IN THE KITCHEN WITH MARY
AND MARTHA: ONE-DISH WONDERS*

Trust God with the Impossible

Years ago, when one of our children was away from the Lord and had reached the point of desperation, the Lord seemed to say to me, "You take care of the possible—and trust Me for the impossible."

— RUTH BELL GRAHAM

The Law of Nature

The law of nature is that a certain quantity of work is necessary to produce a certain quantity of good of any kind whatever. If you want knowledge, you must toil for it; if food, you must toil for it; and if pleasure, you must toil for it.

— JOHN RUSKIN

Abundant Grace

God's chief desire is to reveal Himself to
you and, in order for Him to do that, He
gives you abundant grace.
The Lord gives you the experience of
enjoying His presence. He touches you,
and His touch is so delightful that, more
than ever, you are drawn inwardly to Him.

— MADAME JEANNE GUYON

Fresh and Tender

Indeed, now that I come to think of it,
I never really feel grown-up at all.
Perhaps this is because childhood, catching
our imagination when it is fresh and tender,
never lets go of us.

—J. B. PRIESTLY

Wings

Be like the bird that, halting in its flight
Awhile on boughs too slight,
Feels them give way beneath her, and yet sings
Knowing that she hath wings.

— VICTOR HUGO

Miracle to Miracle

To be alive, to be able to see, to walk, to have a home. . .
it's all a miracle. I have adopted the technique of living life
from miracle to miracle.

— ARTHUR RUBENSTEIN

Elements of Joy

Into all lives, in many simple, familiar,
homely ways, God infuses this element
of joy from the surprises of life,
which unexpectedly brighten our days
and fill our eyes with light.

— HENRY WADSWORTH LONGFELLOW

Your Truest Friend

A mother is the truest friend we have, when trials
heavy and sudden, fall upon us; when adversity
takes the place of prosperity; when friends who
rejoice with us in our sunshine desert us;
when trouble thickens around us, still will she
cling to us, and endeavor by her kind precepts
and counsels to dissipate the clouds of darkness,
and cause peace to return to our hearts.

— WASHINGTON IRVING

Cup of Blessing

Never lose an opportunity of seeing anything that is
beautiful; for beauty is God's handwriting—
a wayside sacrament. Welcome it in every fair face,
in every fair sky, in every fair flower, and thank God
for it as a cup of blessing.

— RALPH WALDO EMERSON

Catch Beauties!

If I have learnt anything, it is that life forms no logical patterns. It is haphazard and full of beauties which I try to catch as they fly by, for who knows whether any of them will ever return?

— MARGOT FONTEYN

Sugar and Spice

What are little girls made of, made of?
What are little girls made of?
Sugar and spice and all things nice.
That's what little girls are made of.

— Nursery Rhyme

A Large Heart

A mother had a slender, small body, but a large heart. . .a heart so large that everybody's grief and everybody's joy found welcome in it, and hospitable accommodation.

—MARK TWAIN

Unity

I must decide to subordinate my will to that of my
heavenly Father. It's the only way my life can have
unity. Without that unity, I'll become fragmented and
my daily decisions will pull me apart at the center.

— MARILYN MORGAN HELLEBERG

Many Things. . .

Families give us many things—love and meaning,
purpose and an opportunity to give,
and a sense of humor.

— UNKNOWN

Perfect Harmony

Clothe yourselves with compassion, kindness, humility, meekness, and patience. Bear with one another and, if anyone has a complaint against another, forgive each other; just as the Lord has forgiven you, so you also must forgive. Above all, clothe yourselves with love, which binds everything together in perfect harmony. And let the peace of Christ rule in your hearts.

— COLOSSIANS 3:12–15 NRSV

A Special Need

If you have a special need today, focus your full attention on the goodness and greatness of your Father rather than on the size of your need. Your need is so small compared to His ability to meet it.

— ANONYMOUS

I Love to Play

I love to play hide-and-seek with my kid, but some days, my goal is to find a hiding place where he can't find me until after high school.

— UNKNOWN

Empower Me

Dear Father, help me to give You everything today:
the things I do well—and the things at which I fail.
Empower me to accept my circumstances, even life's daily
frustrations. Thank You that when I am weak,
You are strong. Amen.

— ELLYN SANNA

Who Do You Love the Best?

"Isn't there one child you really love the best?" a mother was asked. And she replied, "Yes. The one who is sick, until he gets well; the one who's away, until he gets home."

— UNKNOWN

Almond Blossom

My mother's love is the almond blossom of my
mind and the fragrance is worth dying for.
Her gentle compassionate touch shaped my
very essence and I will always attempt to
become the man that she perceived me to be.

—— FRANK L. DE ROOS III

Flaws and All

Ask the Lord to help you see your children as God
sees them. And, ask Him to help you see yourself
through His eyes, too. In other words, give your
kids and yourself a break. Don't expect them to be
perfect, and don't expect perfection from yourself,
either. God loves you and your kids—flaws and all.

— MICHELLE MEDLOCK ADAMS

Holy Love

Even He that died for us upon the cross
was mindful of His mother, as if to teach us that
this holy love should be our last worldly thought.

—— HENRY WADSWORTH
LONGFELLOW

Giving

Giving seems to be the very essence of
motherhood. So many calls in the night,
so many demands in the day, so little time for
oneself, and so much to give. . . .
There is One who gave and who gives more
than any mother. And how mothers need
that which He has to give. . . .

— DORIS COFFIN ALDRICH

All I Am

All I am I owe to my mother. I attribute all my
success in life to the moral, intellectual,
and physical education I received from her.

— GEORGE WASHINGTON

Family

Family are those people you know you will have for
the rest of your life. You're welded together by love,
trust, respect, or loss—or simple embarrassment.

— UNKNOWN

God's Goodness

Stilled now be every anxious care;
See God's great goodness everywhere;
Leave all to Him in perfect rest:
He will do all things for the best.

— UNKNOWN

Angels

The dear angels are not so proud as we human beings are. They walk in obedience to God, serve mankind, and take care of little children. How could they perform a more significant work than taking care of children day and night?

— MARTIN LUTHER

The Best

Our children are faced with many challenges.
Sometimes, we're the only ones believing the
best in them. We're the only ones on their side.
Believing the best in our children doesn't mean
turning our heads when they act inappropriately.
Rather, it means giving them the benefit of the
doubt. If we believe the best in our children,
we'll get the best from our children.

— MICHELLE MEDLOCK ADAMS

Perfectly Safe and Secure

When we are told that God, who is our dwelling place, is also our fortress, it can only mean one thing. . .that if we but live in our dwelling place, we shall be perfectly safe and secure.

— HANNAH WHITALL SMITH

Send Thy Blessing

May young and old together find
in Christ the Lord of every day,
That fellowship our homes may bind
in joy and sorrow, work and play.
Our Father, on the homes we love
Send down thy blessing from above.

— HUGH MARTIN

Great Grace

It is no great matter to associate with the good
and gentle, for this is naturally pleasing to all,
and everyone willingly enjoyeth peace,
and loveth those best that agree with him.
But to be able to live peaceably with hard and
perverse persons, or with the disorderly, or
with such as go contrary to us, is a great grace,
and a most commendable and manly thing.

—— THOMAS À KEMPIS

A Mother Fills a Place

A mother. . .fills a place so great that there isn't an angel in heaven who wouldn't be glad to give a bushel of diamonds to come down here and take her place.

— BILLY SUNDAY

A Mother Who Read to Me

You may have tangible wealth untold;
Caskets of jewels and coffers of gold.
Richer than I you can never be,
I had a mother who read to me.

— STRICKLAND GILLILAN

As I Am

Grace means God accepts me just as I am. He does not require or insist that I measure up to someone else's standard of performance. He loves me completely, thoroughly, and perfectly. There's nothing I can do to add or to detract from that love.

— MARY GRAHAM

All Your Needs

Your heavenly Father already knows all your
needs. Seek the Kingdom of God above all
else, and live righteously, and he will give you
everything you need. So don't worry
about tomorrow.

—— MATTHEW 6:32–34 NLT

Frogs and Snails and Puppy Dog Tails

What are little boys made of, made of?
What are little boys made of?
Frogs and snails and puppy-dogs' tails.
That's what little boys are made of.

— NURSERY RHYME

Never Wasted

Nothing you do for children is ever wasted.
They seem not to notice us, hovering, averting our
eyes, and they seldom offer thanks, but what we do
for them is never wasted.

— GARRISON KEILLOR

Jacob's God

The Reverend Moses Browne had twelve children.
When someone remarked to him, "Sir, you have just as
many children as Jacob," he responded, "Yes, and I have
Jacob's God to provide for them."

— UNKNOWN

A Missing Angel

Thank you, God, for pretending not to notice that one of your angels is missing and for guiding her to me. Sometimes I wonder what special name you had for her. I call her "Mother."

—— BERNICE MADDUX

God's Hand Guides Us

At different times in my life, I have felt His hand guide me to choose wisely in the midst of uncertainty. . . . Those moments have come only when I have been consistent in making time for prayer and consciously seeking His direction for me.

— SHIRLEY DOBSON

Thank You for My Home

Dear Lord, thank You for my home. I ask that You fill it with Your Holy Spirit. Even when I don't have time to polish and dust, may it still shine with Your welcome and love, so that whoever comes in my doors senses that You are present.

— ELLYN SANNA

God's Design

The family is God's design. . . . He gave it His highest endorsement when He placed His own Son within its protective, nurturing walls. Within this framework, His plan for humanity and for Himself will best come to fulfillment.

— JANE HANSEN

The Greatest Difference

The greatest difference which I find between my mother and the rest of the people whom I have known is this, and it is a remarkable one: while others felt a strong interest in a few things, she felt a strong interest in the whole world and everything and everybody in it.

— MARK TWAIN

Peacefulness Brings Healing

When a mother exudes a sense of peace and
tranquility, her family feels calm.
Peacefulness brings healing to a troubled spirit.
A peaceful mother is like a medicinal balm.
Peace and assurance of Mother's love are
necessary ingredients for a happy home.

— Unknown

The Best-Paid Job in the World

We can look at our job as the best-paid one in the world—because we get compensated in ways that other people don't. Just last week, I got a bouquet of cattails, a science fair trophy, three "I missed yous," and lots of sloppy kisses. Would I trade that for stock options, a penthouse office suite, or a lifetime of spa treatments? Not in a million years.

—— DENA DYER

A Perfect Mother

The greatest thing she'd learned over the years was that
there was no way to be a perfect mother,
but a million ways to be a good one.

— UNKNOWN

A Heart Too Big

We find delight in the beauty and happiness of
children that makes the heart too big for the body.

— RALPH WALDO EMERSON

Too Big

God's grace is too big, too great to understand
fully. So we must take the moments of His grace
throughout the day with us; the music of the
songbird in the morning, the kindness shown in
the afternoon, and the restful sleep at night.

— ANONYMOUS

Day 355

The Successful Mother

The successful mother, the mother who does her part in rearing and training aright the boys and girls who are to be the men and women of the next generation, is of greater use to the community. . . . She is more important by far than the successful statesman or businessman or artist or scientist.

— THEODORE ROOSEVELT

The Spirit of Stillness

Do whatever is necessary to nurture the spirit of stillness
in your life. Don't let the enemy wear you so thin that you
lose your balance and perspective. Regular time for stillness
is as important and necessary as sleep, exercise,
and nutritional food.

— EMILIE BARNES

Don't Worry

When we take our prayer requests to God and
then continue to worry, it is as if we are saying,
"Thanks so much for stopping to listen to me,
but I'm not sure You can help."

— SHEILA WALSH

One Hundred Years from Now

A hundred years from now, it will not matter what my bank account was, the sort of house I lived in, or the kind of car I drove. But the world may be different because I was important in the life of a child.

— UNKNOWN

No Interruptions

Turn off the TV, leave the radio off, don't answer the telephone. . . . Make a "no interruptions" rule at the dinner table so you can focus on just being together as a family.

— FROM *IN THE KITCHEN WITH MARY AND MARTHA*

The Best
Six Doctors

The best six doctors anywhere
And no one can deny it
Are sunshine, water, rest, and air
Exercise and diet.
These six will gladly you attend
If only you are willing
Your mind they'll ease
Your will they'll mend
And charge you not a shilling.

— NURSERY RHYME

A Household Name

GOD, brilliant Lord, yours is a household name. Nursing infants gurgle choruses about you; toddlers shout the songs that drown out enemy talk.

— PSALM 8:1–2 MSG

Mothers Are Very Special

Mothers are very special,
they are friends of treasured worth. . .
and one who knows their love
has the greatest gift on earth.

— ANONYMOUS

Sleep in Peace

Have courage for the great sorrows of life and patience for the small ones; and when you have laboriously accomplished your daily task, go to sleep in peace. God is awake.

— VICTOR HUGO

A Rock in a Weary Land

O Lord, who art as the Shadow of a great Rock in a weary
land, who beholdest Thy weak creatures weary of labor,
weary of pleasure, weary of hope deferred,
weary of self; in Thine abundant compassion,
and unutterable tenderness, bring us, I pray Thee,
unto Thy rest. Amen.

— CHRISTINA G. ROSSETTI

Give Us Grace

God, give us grace to accept with serenity the
things that cannot be changed,
courage to change the things that can be
changed, and the wisdom to distinguish one
from the other.

— REINHOLD NIEBUHR

NOTES